LAUDS & NIGHTSOUNDS

Poetry

$3 -

(as is -

flocking)

OTHER BOOKS BY HARVEY SHAPIRO

The Eye (Alan Swallow)
The Book and Other Poems (Cummington Press)
Mountain, Fire, Thornbush (Alan Swallow)
Battle Report (Wesleyan University Press)
This World (Wesleyan University Press)
Lauds (SUN)

Lauds &
Nightsounds

Harvey Shapiro

SUN
New York 1978

ACKNOWLEDGEMENTS

Many of these poems appeared previously in *Antaeus, Bird Effort, Chelsea, Choice, Equal Time, Event, Harper's, Hudson Review, Mulberry, New Letters, New York Arts Journal, Poetry Now, Present Tense, Roy Rogers, Some, Sun, The Nation, The Sou'wester,* and *Undine.* "Vacation Poetry" was published as a broadside by A Poem A Month Club, Inc.

Copyright © 1975, 1978 by Harvey Shapiro

All rights reserved. No part of this publication may be reproduced or transmitted in any form or by any means, electronic or mechanical, including photocopy, recording, or any information storage and retrieval system without the written permission of the publisher, except in the case of brief quotations embodied in critical articles and reviews. For information address SUN, 456 Riverside Drive, New York, N.Y. 10027.

Lauds, the first part of this collection, was originally published by SUN in 1975.

Printed in the United States of America

First Edition

Library of Congress Cataloging in Publication Data

Shapiro, Harvey

Lauds & nightsounds

"Lauds, the first part of this collection, was originally published by Sun in 1975."

I. Title.

PS3537.H264L3   1978   811'.5'2   74-34539
ISBN 0-915342-07-3
ISBN 0-915342-01-4 pbk.

The publication of this book is supported by grants from the National Endowment for the Arts in Washington, D.C., a Federal Agency, and the New York State Council on the Arts.

To the memory of Tom McMahon

CONTENTS

Lauds

Nightsounds

Lauds

THROUGH THE BOROUGHS

I hear the music from the street
Every night. Sequestered at my desk,
My luminous hand finding the dark words.
Hard, very hard. And the music
From car radios is so effortless.
And so I strive to join my music
To that music. So that
The air will carry my voice down
The block, across the bridge,
Through the boroughs where people I love
Can hear my voice, saying to them
Through the music that their lives
Are speaking to them now, as mine to me.

NOTES AT 46

1. What distinguishes our work
    Is an American desperation.
    Who thought to find this
    In the new world?

2. I owe my father a tribute.
    On his last day
    When the head nurse
    Asked what he wanted
    He said, I want to
    Look into the eyes of a young girl.

    The eyes of a young girl.
    I want to look into
    The eyes of a young girl.

3. It's nothing to me
    Who gathers us in.
    And it's nothing to me
    Who owns us now.

    I can think of Venice
    Or Jerusalem.

    Armand's little goat beard
    Quivers in the spring.

4. It suddenly strikes me
That at forty-six
I want to write the lyrics
Of a boy of twenty
So I blow my brains out.

5. Not wanting to invent emotion
I pursued the flat literal,
Saying wife, children, job
Over and over.
When the words took on
Emotion I changed their order.
In this way, I reached daylight
About midnight.

6. "I wish I had never been born!"
He shouts at six.
A pure despair.
At forty-six I cannot say that
With honesty.
Pure passion is beyond me.
Everything is mixed.
Grief allied with joy—
That he is able to say it!

7. In October the house is chill.
Still, the cricket of summer
Sings, reminding us of promises.
As long as the heart listens
It pumps blood.

RIDING WESTWARD

It's holiday night
And crazy Jews are on the road,
Finished with fasting and high on prayer.
On either side of the Long Island Expressway
The lights go spinning
Like the twin ends of my tallis.
I hope I can make it to Utopia Parkway
Where my father lies at the end of his road.
And then home to Brooklyn.
Jews, departure from the law
Is equivalent to death.
Shades, we greet each other.
Darkly, on the Long Island Expressway,
Where I say my own prayers for the dead,
Crowded in Queens, remembered in Queens,
As far away as Brooklyn. Cemeteries
Break against the City like seas,
A white froth of tombstones
Or like schools of herring, still desperate
To escape the angel of death.
Entering the City, you have to say
Memorial prayers as he slides overhead
Looking something like my father approaching
The Ark as the gates close on the Day of Atonement
Here in the car and in Queens and in Brooklyn.

FOR THE YIDDISH SINGERS IN THE LAKEWOOD HOTELS OF MY CHILDHOOD

I don't want to be sheltered here.
I don't want to keep crawling back
To this page, saying to myself,
This is what I have.

I never wanted to make
Sentimental music in the Brill Building.
It's not the voice of Frank Sinatra
I hear.

To be a Jew in Manhattan
Doesn't have to be this.
These lights flung like farfel.
These golden girls.

IN BROOKLYN HARBOR

In Brooklyn harbor
The last light hits the tugs
And Battery shines,
And no one wants to
Make the City any more.
"The Oriental Warrior"
Riding in the bay.

Gulls between the sun
And Governors Island.
Jehovah's Watchtower
With the Squibb tripos
Ever golden. We play
Basketball in the park
Along the harbor. The Bridge
Still stands, getting ancient
With its freight of poetry.

"JESUS, MARY I LOVE YOU SAVE SOULS"

IRT graffiti
For the five o'clock rush hour.
Souls in the car.
Carrying you in my head.
Your head thrown back,
Legs parted. Jesus, Mary
Save souls. I love you.
When we get
To the dark part
Of the ride, under the river,
Keep me in that light,
Subway car light,
Burning forever
With that image
In my brain.

FOR THE SPARROWS
ON NEW YEAR'S MORNING

Resolved that I will help feed you in your ivy
And listen for you in the streets
Now that I have heard you, first sound of the year
After the harbor hootings. This morning,
Blurred as the ends of sleep,
You make my resolutions clear, touching on song:
To celebrate without cause whenever
I can put words to sense and music.
And to whoever hears me, let her know
I listen to sparrows.

DISTANCES

She has a kind of grainy beauty
Like one of those square-thumbed,
Slab-footed Greek maidens of
Picasso. So when I see her
I think of sand and sea.

My life on the empty beaches
Just starting to come back.
All the way home we sang
Songs of the 40's and 50's —
"Reeked with class" —
And the kids broke up.
Sometimes they worry
About the desperate way I drive.

There are these distances.

TRUE

It's true I shed tears
In my forties, suddenly,
Explaining who I was
Or where I had been.
Almost like my children,
Who I am quick to comfort.
But I let them
Taste their tears.
The years have taught me.

SAUL'S PROGRESS

1.

I told my son:
"Stop trying to screw the monkey's tail
Into his bellybutton.
Originality
Is never its own
Justification.
Some innovations
Get nowhere."

"The Sunday monkeys are my friends,"
He said.
I was on my way down
From the heavenly city
Of the 18th Century philosophers.
He was on his way up,
Almost three.

2.

"Moby Dick is smarter than
The other dicks."
A song to make the
Bad guys happy.
You sang it all day Saturday
With snot-filled nose
And clouded eye,
To raise me
To a fury.

3.

You sit on the crest of a dune
Facing the sea,
Which is beyond sight.
Your anger at me
Makes you play by yourself,
Tell stories to yourself,
Fling out your hurt
To the wide sky's healing.
A red boat in one hand,
A blue in the other,
You begin singing songs
About the weather.
Cliff swallow, brilliant skimmer.

4.

As if he were me, he comes bounding in,
All happiness. I owe him
All happiness. For these years at least.
When he smiles and says, a good time,
I have no notion who else
He has made happy with my happiness.

BRINGING UP KIDS

He goes into paroxysms of grief.
I am baffled by his non-communication,
Knowing perfectly well everything
His rage means to the shaking house.
Disorder at night. It is natural.
He wants to know why it is right.

VETERAN

1.

I never thought I'd be a survivor
And base everything on that strategy.
Closing in on fifty, almost un-American,
Out of it, I'm close to myself again
In my fifty-mission photo—
Poised in leather jacket, parachute harness,
By the twin guns of the bomber—
Breathing now,
Twenty, numb, a survivor.

2.

To open myself to the wars,
The TV newsreels,
The savage fighting.
To walk with this knowledge,
To see light in this light.
Which was my own youngness.
The shell exploding under the fuselage.
Smoke drifting through the cabin.
Hearing the shell, smelling the smoke.
Knowing it is fire. Making that knowledge
Be with me in the everyday.
Opening my eyes to the sunlight,
Frozen, the condition of my will.
Looking through that to my childhood,
My children.

3.

Frozen and baffled,
There is nothing
To be gained
From searching that time.
If one had an answer —
How use it?
Instead, there is the victory
Of being here
With what one has
Like the world itself
That lives
Through time.

EVERY DAY

It's my own dread existence
Stalking me now with a spiritual fury
Like some beast from
Twenty thousand fathoms down
Rammed into the world by events
I seem not to have noticed.

MUSE POEM

While I'm waiting for the words,
Could you just
Lean over me a little,
That way,
With your breasts
Of imagination, incense,
And blue dawns.

It is always the same quiet night.
You in your desperation say,
"What you are writing is poetry.
No one will read it."
You worry about my health
When I find I am not
To be famous. But I am
Already inside you in my thoughts.

LOW KEY

Strategies of poetry.
They demand that we stay in a low key.
How else could I sleep, rise, go to work?
But to bang my head against the wall.
To lie down on the pavement
And hit my head against it.
Like that boy I saw, years ago,
On his sixteenth birthday.
Because the world wouldn't let him in.
Because I touched your breasts
And cannot make a world out of that touch.
That was Wednesday, now it's Friday.

IN THE ROOM

Seeing the figure of that man
Caught in a murderous hatred,
I wept for him openly
Before the children,
And I write of him in a low style
But touching on elevated things.

In the room
Nothing has happened
Yet the two of them
Stand apart, watching a ship
Wreck, a wild storm,
Their own blood drumming.

Her hatred of him
Makes her eyes shine,
Brings color to the points
Of her fingers and her hair.

Before we knew about urban poetry
I opened the door and found you
Bathing in the sink, on Stanton Street—
1949—your skin still gleaming.

I can't sleep.
Love has fixed my head.
Now this girl, now that.

Who needs this tumult?
I ask myself,
So proud of the hours
I spend staring.

Muse,
Once you made this chaos shine.

ARRIVING

The way tunnel workers got the bends
In Warner Bros. movies
I am caught
In the tensions of you.

Describing
Walt Frazier's play
The kid says
So many moves!
And I think of you
In our last season.

Here I am, with
An armful of platitudes
At your door. That
You are never in
Makes my style.

MONTAUK HIGHWAY

Murderous middle age is my engine.

A NOTEBOOK

At the bare edge
The images seem fabulous.

I certainly didn't
Wear myself out
With brilliance.

"It is forbidden to be old" (Nachman).

If you steam blast the bricks
In Brooklyn, they will
Come up as bright as Henry James.

Dead Indians are in the underbrush
Waiting for the word.

I don't like you
And I don't know
Anyone else.

The stars be hid
That led me to this pain.

I stroke my wife's angel hair
Thinking of you.

It is a bowl of blue light.
It will be there all day
Now that I have seen it.

I take out my old anxieties
And they still work.

A notebook of dry cunts.

Why is everything discussed
With that high cackle?
Ladies, I weep for beauty
And you bear it.

I used to visit bombed out towns.
Now I visit bombed out people.
There's a kind of beautiful smell
To both, which I can't
Put out of my mind.

Man, the master of choice.

Words, rushing into judgment.

All right, you mother stickers,
This is a fuck up.

IN OUR DAY

Society
Turning its past
To glorious junk,
Like the artist,
In our day.
Free-floating
Liberation
As a style
In the street.
Everybody
Playing
In the muck
Of the imagination,
Finger-painting
The walls
For psychic health.
The mind's rigor
Become
A sunlit field.

HOW DIFFERENCES ARISE

He thinks we live in Rome
Before the coming of Caesar.
He worries about
The health of the Republic.
I know we live in China
Sometime before the coming
Of Confucius.
I find his ideas ridiculous.

1971

The radiators
Driven to madness
By the ascending steam
Want to open
Their valves forever.

Nearing the end
Of a century
Everybody smiles.

JANIS

Seeing you again
I cried for the time
I spent, misspent,
In the rain,
Drinking the booze of confusion.
Ah you, and your ball and chain.
Heels lifted, tugging
At my sentimental heart
Like I was your big daddy
Who wasn't there.
I did drop tears for you.
I was so deep into you,
Coming out of my own generation.
Poster art is what
The pansy said we were all about.
American tears for thee.

YEARS

In the traffic outside the window
Ella Fitzgerald's voice—
A car radio at 2 AM—
Like all those years
Coming þack, coming back
Zoom, they're gone, with the traffic,
With the voice. The jazz of that time
Riding out the nothing war,
The nothing books, the nothing years.

READING AT A GHETTO SCHOOL

Against the cutting edge
Of their reality,
My reality.
Against their violence,
My violence.
Against their language,
My ability to pick up the gun.

ADAPTATION OF A FIRST GRADE
COMPOSITION

I supposed I used you
The way an Indian used his buffalo.

I have come in your queenly cunt,
Your tight asshole of an Indian princess.

Buffalo skin for the tepees,
Blankets, pants, and moccasins.
Bones to make tools and drumsticks.
Teeth to make necklaces and anklets.
Skulls to make masks.
And they ate the buffalo meat.

SO I CALL YOU

I am like a schoolboy
Winning prizes.
Then I call you
And no one answers.

I am on so many
Useless errands,
Can I single out this one
And call it glory?

In the tent of your hair
I sleep an entire night.

Alone, the phone in my hand,
The words in my head,
Ringing, ringing.

IN FEAR OF FAILURE

1.

Facing myself in a long corridor.
A hotel, shoes outside every door.
The light steady, so I can't tell
If it is day or night.
Myself coming toward me,
Murder in the eyes,
The hands trying to form an instrument.
And I sit here before the keys
Remembering when the letters
Were instruments of creation.

2.

I see you stand
In the presence of the nouns,
The great shining of the worlds.
You who are as far from me
As thought.

As if a door had been opened
That I could not
Keep open.
Even so
I write the words.

3.

Opening the matches
On my desk I read "Your instructor
Is but minutes away."
I sit patiently
Pen in hand
Though it is only
The U.S. Auto Club
Addressing me
And I've been
Driving unsuccessfully
For twenty years.

4.

If a world
Still exists
Lights flashing
Like a city
Or a great ship
Going down.

5.

I wake from the images.
I have been sleeping with a girl
Half my age. In the light
The engines are moving the day
Into position.

6.

Telling the way
One has gone oneself
Or describing a way
Which leads there.

If that will help us.

Complete darkness.

7.

The rain for its own sake
So slowly on the roof,
Easing the world,
Even my own anger.
And a solitary bird
Near the house keeps
Telling me what he needs
To tell me: Your drama
Has been played out.

FOR THE YEAR'S END

Staying indoors
At the year's end.
The garden still so green
Against the brick.
The young willow
Set in the cold air
Like an open hand.
Music
Driving me to the year's end,
Which I choose,
Turn to now, wanting
To be in
These streets
By the river and the bridge.
I can hardly understand
What holds the music.
A city
Above the water.
Stone holding the music.
Ivy on the wall
In winter.

CITY PORTRAIT

Her husband didn't give her highs,
Just made her lows less low.
Said, with the lips trembling.
Breasts too, I think.
Beautiful woman.
Going to bed with strangers now.
Trying to think it all out.
On the west side of Manhattan,
Twelve floors above the murderous streets.

VIEWS OF HER

1.

The pornographic peepshow in my head.
Her dark hair flowing like the music.

The small trembling begins
Throughout her entire body.
Hands dangling into nothingness.
Her cheeks wet with tears.

2.

I imagine
Making love to you
In your butterfly sweatshirt.
(How alert of me
To have noticed that.)
The wings take us up
And bring us back.

3.

She's moon-laden.
She's deep
In the tides,
With her ass
Like a sand bar
Or a summer hotel.

4.

Why I could not
Have you (in your
Purple dress)
You never said so that
It made sense to me.

You are only
A disturbance
In my brain.

5.

Her beauty has hit me.
I wanted to calm down.
Everyone else was going crazy.
I could see that was a way
But was it the right way.
Being calm
I could think about it.
Her beauty has hit me.

6.

Saying, I think you're beautiful,
Doesn't mean much. You've
Heard it before, I've said it before.
But I believe there was
Justice in it every time I said it.
I have to be the man who lived
The life that brought me here.

LAUDS

I can see by your
Rosy nipples
You are the goddess of the dawn.

A GIFT

She made him a gift of her touch,
Softly turning the collar of his jacket down
In the crowded elevator. To say,
See, my spirit still hovers to protect.

That he could prize such useless moments.

Motorbikes break the night's silence.
The President's face on the television screen.
Green on my set. Words muffling perception.
Everything keeps us from the truth, which
Begins to have a religious presence.
Why so many claim it, in the tail of the tiger
Or elsewhere. No matter. When I find it,
Being so rare, it is fiercer than whiskey.
My eyes burn with happiness and I speak
Collected into myself.

LIKE A BEACH

Even the unlived life within us
Is worth examining.
Maybe it is all we have.
The rest is burned up
Like fuel in the furnace.
But the unlived life
Stretches within us like a beach.
There is a gull's shadow on it.
Or it is at night and the moon
Crusts the sand.
Or it is a house at night
With people talking in the next room
Over cards.
                    You believe
In these observations?
Doesn't the sea sweep in,
The action begin in the house
At night, the voices of the players
Loud in argument,
Their motives, their needs,
Turbulent as the sea?
Whose happiness
Even here
Is being sacrificed?

AUGUST

Ancient mariner, your gray beard
Dries in the sun, salt sparkling
The wires. Beached on this vacation coast,
You have forgotten your story.
It's drifted away among children,
Scrub pine, the chattering sea.
And there is no one to hold
By the eye or sweet tit anyway.
Better to whistle with the birds
And pick berries in the sun.

SUMMER

1.

The beach was so cuntish
The fog could hardly fill
All the little crevices.

2.

The half moon at the end of the street.
Little half moon, making this a village.
Streets of no light and of pure shadow.

3.

Emotional catbirds.

4.

Ted Roethke
Would sit under a tree
With refrigerated wine,
A carton of poetry books,
And his notebook to turn
To when the sweat rose.

5.

Master brother sun,
In my own canticle of all created things

(Beatle music coming from the house
As I sit with this pad
In the burnished grass) your praise
Would be first, also, and by due:
Poetry is your spin-off.

In your morning blaze,
I seem to see the compacted elements
Flare singly clear. But for sister
Our bodily death, the end
Of the song, let the saint praise her.
I hold hard to my cigar,
Watching the smoke eddy out
Through the leaves
Of the sheltering oak.

6.

I can begin to taste my life.
The wine's sweet influence.
Surf or traffic, I can't tell.
When you begin, stars cluster on the vine.
You walk through a meadow.
You stand casting from an open boat
Into Scorpio. Soft chalk
In the sky because it is mid August
And the time of Perseids.
Now am I home in Helicon,
The real estate I was meant to keep.

MUSICAL SHUTTLE

Night, expositor of love.
Seeing the sky for the first time
That year, I watched the summer constellations
Hang in air: Scorpio with
Half of heaven in his tail.
Breath, tissue of air, cat's cradle.
I walked the shore
Where cold rocks mourned in water
Like the planets lost in air.
Ocean was a low sound.
The gate-keeper suddenly gone,
Whatever the heart cried
Voice tied to dark sound.
The shuttle went way back then,
Hooking me up to the first song
That ever chimed in my head.
Under a sky gone slick with stars,
The aria tumbling forth:
Bird and star.
However those cadences
Rocked me in the learning years,
However that soft death sang —
Of star become a bird's pulse,
Of the spanned distances
Where the bird's breath eddied forth —
I recovered the lost ground.

The bird's throat
Bare as the sand on which I walked.
Love in his season
Had moved me with that song.

Nightsounds

TIGHT LIKE THAT

Who can refuse to live his own life?
A spray of leaves in the lamplight.
A saxophone on the dark street.
Like the forties. In those days
For the price of a pitcher of beer
You could spend Saturday afternoon
Listening to the exchanges,
The deep guttural stirrings
Of so much light and dark.
At the corner of fifty-second
At the break at the Downbeat
We saw Billie draped in fur,
Gardenia in her hair.
Bless you, children, she said.
Whatever became of the music
I drank to at Nick's bar,
Pee Wee Russell's clarinet
Jammed into Brunes's belly,
Shaking like his sister Kate.
Hunkering down into my own story,
I begin to see it all close up,
Just under the pavement.

THE BRIDGE
for John Wissemann

John, the old bunker fleet at Greenport
Is a ghost. Many beautiful things are gone.
The masts, the dockside buildings
Float in your blue water colors,
Blue and black, in Brooklyn,
Where I seem to be giving up the ghost.
Artists of the region. All one island.
Whitman's crummy fish-shaped island.

Like you I do the indigenous stuff—
Crabs from the creek, blues from the September sea,
Poems from the tar roofs and the redbrick library
Where they house the prints—opening the Bridge!
Fireworks and exultation! Crowds moving
In a mighty congress back and forth.
While we, unmoving on the starry grid of America,
Stare failure in the face, our blazing star.

It was a dream of summer. From the cliffs above
The Sound—humming birds hovering, red foxes
At the door—at evening I could see the schools
Of blues come in, savaging the waters and the bait.
Everything I wrote was magic to me. Ancient days.
Believe me, John, they wear us down with shit and work.
But one pure line—still mine or yours
For the grasping—can take us to that farther shore.

LOSS

The Union Street Bridge
Spans (in three steps)
The Gowanus Canal.
I had no notion of community
Crossing it, cursing those
On this side, then the other.
The tenements in a rose-red light.
The stoops and petty alibis.
The Gowanus flaking red,
Dead water. My heart
Was in my mouth once again.
Drive the car was all I knew.
I could ricochet from shore
To shore of America,
High on sunsets,
Honoring the poets.
Not enough.

NOW

The house smells of young cunt. Laughter
In the upstairs hall. Age weighs on me
As I sit through it. My son's quick step
Hurrying over me to the john.

IN THE HOUSE

1.

I have these visitors:
Dog and cat.
My way of relating to God.
Crying, they come to me
To be assured'of my presence.
Whatever their natures, they have this need,
Which I can satisfy,
Putting a hand on their throat.

2.

As if I were my own enemy
I eat clippings of my hair, beard and nails
And go forth to seize the house,
Wife and job of the man I have
Inhabited. Ashes in my mouth.

3.

Playing the lyre of the spirit
In Brooklyn
On a winter night,
Animals about me,
The house asleep,
The tree of life
Swaying as I play
Outside my window
In the sodium glare.

EVERYTHING SMELLS A LITTLE LIKE METAL AND FAREWELL

(Louise Bogan in a letter)

And if there is no lust to respond to,
What can a woman make of the world.
Waking at five to the sound of gulls
Over the harbor and the bridge. My world
Of the subways and ticking towers. To which
I offer the response of memories, dreams.
A second generation hurrying through the streets
After my father's ghost. Wondering why
Why in America is this the way we live.
Alone in her glassed-in apartment, facing the park,
The lights, luxurious thighs offered up
As a setting, food, drink, the delights
Of the eye, of touch, dark hair draping
A bedroom, a city. And she had come back
From crying at her shrink's. Over what?
Routine crying, a sense of loss. Remembering how
I could not taste the real, there or in the
streets
Or at work, facing the harbor, sound of gulls breaking . . .

INCIDENT

1.

Tremendous pleasure lurking in my skin.
You stretch, your small breasts announcing,
This is the beginning. If we were to lie together,
I would have to tell you my long story.
Slowly I begin to rehearse it.

2.

As a flame is joined to a coal.
That cleaving to the source.
I don't hear from you for ten days.
Still, everyone says I look good.

3.

It's your cunt, and your
Voice. But nobody
Owns the language.

4.

Gift of the season.
In the dark of the year,
Over her mouth
And eyes her own
Hair shapes her.

Sternly she said to me,
We must have a discussion.
Meaning, I surmised,
No more of her hair over her eyes.
The saliva with which
She fixes her contact lenses
No longer to ease my lines.

5.

I passed you
Standing at the rail
In the Indianapolis
Speedway of my bankrupt emotions,
Going into the last turn
Before the blossoming fire.
It made me want to pull out.
That's me, waving thanks to you,
From under the car.

IN THE BROAD STREET

They put their eczema in the sun,
Arms and scalps hanging loose in the broad street.
The hope for healing, never very distant
From this populace. If one had to define their politics,
It would be this. Easter, the sun risen
On the slowly-abandoned city. They are prepared
To give it all away, having nothing. Tropical music
For the carnival, carried at the ready.
Mused the old Jew, when Elijah's face
Appears on the screen, between the commercials,
Who of us will not open the door?

47TH STREET

In the delicatessen
The countermen
Were bantering about the messiah,
Lifting the mounds of corned beef
And tongue. He wouldn't come,
They said, you couldn't
Count on it. Meaning:
They would die in harness.

IN THE SYNAGOGUE

The new year. Five thousand what?
God's deliberate flatness
In his scrolls, with touches of
Megalomania and song.

BROOKLYN GARDENS

Forsythia, scraggly in the backyard.
Crocuses, stabs of blue in the shadow.
Sentiment, blundering now like the trucks.
Even in myself I see mysterious purposes.

THE

The pussy-whipping
Sweetness of an
American romance.

Whatever you do
When you're through
Press me there.

NIGHTSOUNDS

1. The joy of her hair
    On his cock
    Lit up the whole morning.

2. My fingers bear the marks
    Of fish hooks, puppy bites,
    All the sweet bites of the actual.

    You, goddess, who grab me
    Between the second drink and the third,
    I now see like me
    For the marks I carry on me.

3. As if the night were a problem
    I had to crack
    To let the dawn through.

4. It is near bedtime
    And suddenly I am stunned
    By the gold
    Of the whiskey in my glass.
    I cannot understand
    Why so much has been given.

5. He was looking for a
    Universal message like,
    Hemorrhoid sufferers
    You are not alone.

6. You throw one leg
    Over the covers.
    A gleam of snatch
    In the half light.

7. I have long been a man
    Of filthy habits.
    And now in middle age
    They give me pleasure.

8. I am watching another
    Man's defeat.
    It seems
    He cannot bring himself
    To it
    While I watch.

9. Where you stand
    There stand all the worlds.

10. What is this sweetness
    I am overcome by
    As if I had earned
    My rest.

AROUND ME AND INSIDE ME

Every man lives his life
Against some question
If he lives at all.

To make this world perfect and full of splendor,
Was this indeed anybody's wish?
I look around me and inside me.

In my own night head
Drinking slowly, smoking slowly,
The city at my back.
Both of us making
The long recovery to morning.

FATHER AND SONS

If you tell them something truthful
About themselves or about life,
Coming across it
In the middle of a rambling discourse,
How solemn their faces grow.

DOMESTIC MATTERS

1.

It wasn't what I had thought —
Children taking up
Most of the house, leaving
Me (or so it often seems)
Only room enough
For the bed. Which itself
Is a kind of relic, as if
From an earlier
Marriage. And so you turn
In the bedroom door,
White, and so small,
To say goodnight.
To say there are
Two of us.

2.

I am crying over this body of yours
Which is to wither in the dust.
Already your belly's thrust outpoints
Your breasts. The hair of your head
Grows thin. A skeleton
Smiles to me with your gums.

3.

We are almost
Out of earshot
Of one another
Yet our answers
Seem to find
Connected questions
Of an urgency
So deep, they might
Be coming
From the center
Of a life.

4.

We were comrades
In a disastrous war.
We have created a history
That will be sung
In the psyche of others.
Troy's burning
And the flames may light us
All the way to death.

CRY OF THE SMALL RABBITS

The cry of the small rabbits facing death.
Nobody would want to sing like that.
A short, high wailing. So what
If death gave them voice to sing?
I face my own rage and fear, tearing for words
That I can say calmly in sentences
That will not stop. I want to see
The next line glitter, and the last
Come crashing like surf.

BUT THIS IS STRANGE

But this is strange
That even here, in this world,
We can find the images.

The way the Japanese,
Pushed into their subways,
Are aware of centuries
Of images.
            Mist on a lake
In the polluted sky
Over Tokyo.

FOR THE ZEN MASTER SKATEBOARDING DOWN INDEPENDENCE PASS

The upturned soles of Buddha's feet.
He was not himself anymore.
That happiness.

Mind-racing
The green hills, blue
Mountain daisies.

Freedom of the downward glide,
Swallows' wings, overdrive.
Knees bent for the turn
As the mountain turns.

MUFFDIVING ON THE UPPER WEST SIDE

Not only was I there, in the rooms,
But when night cradled those bodegas
I saw the music ripple like stars.

O SEASONS

1.

It seemed reasonable to expect an answer.
That was an early feeling, like owning something.

Urban dawn, and yet to hear the birds.
I must have that happiness.

2.

Speculations about man's soul:
A face within a face,
The transformer, the perfecting agent
In the disassembled gear I carry
With me into day. Crossing the street
Steam flurries from the underground.
My life as hidden as the godhead
On 43rd and Broadway where garments
Of light wrap the tall buildings
And I step forth, fierce to know.

3.

Excuse this boy from life
I wanted my mother to write
As I went off to school.
It would take a cosmic jubilee
To make my soul ascend
From this despair. If I could say
My native home, and turn
In that direction, glass in hand,

Crossing the crowded room
As once I came to you.
These misinformed meditations
Hurrying the world's
Return to waste and void.

4.

So I come home
And the faggot next door
Is singing Hawaiian songs
In a contralto. His job
Must be as tough as mine.

5.

It's true I was timid
On my way to Esau in the Sixties.
Someone said, "The place to which we are going
Is not subject to any law,
Because all that is on the side of death;
But we are going to life." It was
Her heart-shaped ass made me do it.
Descriptions of wreckage. The blown windows
Of a town house in Manhattan.
Fucking in the desert.

6.

Wind in the leaves along the street.
Another year is hurried to its close.

Today I passed a man struck down
On 33rd street. Yesterday,
On the steps of the Borough Hall station
I saw another gone, eyes open
To the sifting, grayish light.

7.

Bordering on vacancy at the year's end.
The whole continent unpeopled.
The created uncreate. The monuments
Crawled back into cold stone. The thick husks.
One thousand nine hundred and seventy-seven
Years of christendom, dumb in this believer,
Cherishing the light to come on the bleak
Cityscape—vacant lot on the street
To Jehovah's Kingdom, by the peerless bridge.

AUTOBIOGRAPHY

1.

It is a dream
Interpreted
Within a dream.
And it shall come
To pass
As a life lived.

2.

I was trained in war.
At nineteen I could put together
A fifty-caliber machine gun
Blindfolded. I do not
Question the utility of art
And hope to do something
Commensurate.

3.

That's real terror,
We say, nodding brightly.

ANCIENT DAYS

Great things had happened.
They felt called upon
To bear witness.
The words, in themselves,
Became events.

YOU YOUNG

It's true now the decisions
Are difficult. Especially
As to identity. How you would
Have liked Germany in the forties
When you knew if
You were SS or Jew.

1976

Vision floats
Over the death camps.
That stink. Till the end
Of history. Not soteriology
Or the American sublime
Can raise man up,
Magnified and sanctified.
The fallen sparks,
Husks, on the street corners,
In the streets.

CONVERSATIONAL

In this family one is not allowed
To say anything carelessly, to get on
A train of thought just to see where it's going.
Example: today I said too bad
I hadn't stayed in the Army;
I'd be retired now, in a small house
In Key West. The family hooted.
You'd be dead. Anyway, you can't stand authority.
You don't know the Army or yourself.
True, all true.
Still, I wish I were
Drunk and in bed in Key West
With the sun making the whole sea
Red from here to Cuba.

PORTRAIT

At forty-six,
His wife committed again,
His two children
Only babes, he couldn't
Even contemplate divorce.
Yet the women were there—
Young women, the wealth
Of the city. He worked
At his job, still dreaming
Of the novel. Saloon dreams,
He said, Irish, you can't
Live without them.

POETS & COMICS

To make a little noise before death.

THE REALIZATION

If one could follow a man
Through the places of his exile,
Asking him at each point
Why he had strayed from his life
Or been turned from it,
In time the dialogue
Would be meaningless
For the exile would be the life.
So we live.

THE OLD WIFE

What he needs
Are six call girls
Each with her own
Cocksucking techniques.
Meanwhile, he brings me
His laundry.

VACATION POETRY

1.

An inexhaustible day but in the end
There were no prizes. I sharpened
Into seeing a few times, before
And after whiskey. The beach was
One great sunlit navel.
The sea, like a medieval gloss, moved
On four levels. I walked east along
The tide mark, the spent text.

2.

This air is made of bird calls,
Telephone wires, blue sky and clouds.
It has a disarming honesty. Peanut butter
Would not spread as evenly.
I have come to think of my day dreams of you,
Seventeen porno movies with one plot,
As a waste of time. The longitudes
Of my indifference begin to envelope space.

3.

How difficult it is to acknowledge
This is what I'm here for. A furniture
Mover might have a stronger sense of mission.
In combat I understood the value of survival
And the necessity for strict attention.

In life's miasma, I drift apart.
Even when she looks toward me
My moves tend to be comical.

4.

"The great elementary principle of pleasure"
By which man "knows and feels, and lives, and moves."
I'll drink to that, said Brustein,
Smacking his lips. For the fourth time today
I swim in the sea. Butterflies pass me
On my bike, as do bikinied women,
Strutting in their cream and brown. Voluptuous
Pages from Keats and Baudelaire.

DITCH PLAINS

To be there when day breaks on the sea's reaches.
The full moon still hung there. At Ditch Plains,
For example, before the surfers appear.
Water over rock and gravel. Shingle sound.
Beautiful enough in this end of July
Drought of fish to make me stand there,
Hungry for a text—in the water, on the sand.
Something to bring back to my desk like
Beach glass or polished stone. I want
My happiness to be visible.
I want to bless this day with meaning.
Let the rest of my life take care of itself
So long as it can hover there.

AFTER DARK

Day's end. The promise of day ended.
A rehearsal to say goodnight.
But peaceably so, after whiskey or love.
Not after pain, not often after pain.

LINES

Blue darkening. A bar of it.
Dan calls to say he'll be home by ten;
Do I mind if he's out that late.
I smoke a cigar, study the page,
Cherish the silence. My paint-
Smeared pants pronounce me
The captain of good works.
Happy homesteader, husband.
So I never trafficked in guns
In Africa. And I became myself
And not another. My own vacillations
Rampant in my lines.
Responsibility on my abraded shoulders.
Singer of neurasthenia, or something like it,
Was my aim. What wings touch
Me now out of the darkening blue?

BROOKLYN STREETS

Verlaine's Paris rain
On the Brooklyn streets,
Slick with sentiment.

Someone walking
Home, 2:30 in the
Morning, like an old song.

THE INTENSITY

When you think over what she said and what you said
The spaces begin to get larger until they modulate
Into silence. You stand there staring at each other
With no balloons floating the words, no
Captions, only the intensity of sight making
A language to scare anyone interested in communication
Or believing that two human beings can connect.

Which is why my happiness on the subway brings me back
To myself after last night's trouble. The body warmth,
The distended-with-sleep faces, the memories
Of Hart Crane riding this line, tunneling this way
Under the river that is east. Next time
When I beg for something, will you recognize
Need, stop talking, stop closing the door.

HAPPINESS IN DOWNTOWN BROOKLYN

This morning
Twenty gospel singers
Roared inside my head.

Happiness
In downtown Brooklyn.

All the solid buildings
Were as bright as clouds.

ANOTHER DAY

This is just another wasted day.
No trees, no flowers, no sweet songs.
The family says I'm at fault.
So does God.
The Muse says, eat me.

FROM A CHINESE MASTER

1.

If you want to enter the room
You have to say something. You cannot
Take it for granted that you have already
Entered the room. This I want
To point out to you with a smile.

2.

Early Sunday. Under the phosphor glare
Birds sing merrily, twigs bud.
A dream pushed me from my bed
Breathing of promise like this April.
Believe me, said the teacher in my dream,
A single true gesture, if it be
Only that of the big toe, is enough.

3.

The glamor of death is on their heads.
Wanderers in the anthologies.
After the job I sit with beer and bourbon.
In what cold light shall we be one?

4.

At the start and at the finish
What we want
Is to be close to the living,
Our heads against the skin of the song.